27 CHRISTMAS SONG LYRICS

Christmas lullaby

Osuagwu Malachy

ISBN: 9798352181393

Cover design by: Art Painter
Library of Congress Control Number: 2018675309
Printed in the United States of America

DEDICATION

To all Christmas lovers, the children, the adults, the adolescent, the aged. To our Lord Jesus Christ whom we celebrate on this day.

CONTENTS

- ✓ HARK! THE HERALD ANGELS SING
- ✓ THE GRINCH THEME SONG
- ✓ I SAW MOMMY KISSING SANTA
- ✓ CLAUS ROCKIN' AROUND THE CHRISTMAS TREE
- ✓ SILENT NIGHT
- ✓ THE FIRST
- ✓ NOEL
- ✓ FELIZ NAVIDAD
- ✓ FROSTY THE SNOWMAN
- ✓ O COME ALL YE FAITHFUL IT'S
- ✓ THE MOST WONDERFUL TIME OF THE YEAR A
- ✓ HOLLY JOLLY CHRISTMAS

About The Author

CHRISTMAS

Christmas, Christian festival celebrating the birth of Jesus.

The English term *Christmas* ("mass on Christ's day") is of fairly recent origin. The earlier term *Yule* may have derived from the Germanic *jōl* or the Anglo-Saxon *geōl*, which referred to the feast of the winter solstice. The corresponding terms in other languages—*Navidad* in Spanish, *Natale* in Italian, *Noël* in French—all probably denote nativity.

The German word *Weihnachten* denotes "hallowed night." Since the early 20th century, Christmas has also been a secular family holiday, observed by Christians and non-Christians alike, devoid of Christian elements, and marked by an increasingly elaborate exchange of gifts. In this secular Christmas celebration, a mythical figure named Santa Claus plays the pivotal role.

The traditionally Christian holiday is a celebration of the birth of the baby Jesus in Bethlehem to Joseph and the Virgin Mary.

The English term "Christmas" **comes from the combination of the words "mass" and "Christ,"**

SONG LYRICS

AWAY IN A MANGER

Away in a manger, no crib for a bed,
The little Lord Jesus laid down his sweet head.

The stars in the sky looked down where he lay,
The little Lord Jesus asleep in the hay.

The cattle are lowing, the baby awakes,
But little Lord Jesus no crying he makes.

I love Thee, Lord Jesus, look down from the sky
And stay by my cradle 'til morning is nigh.

Be near me, Lord Jesus, I ask Thee to stay
Close by me forever, and love me, I pray.

Bless all the dear children in thy tender care,
And take us to heaven, to live with Thee there.

DECK THE HALLS

Deck the halls with boughs of holly, Fa la la la la la la la!

'Tis the season to be jolly, Fa la la la la la la la!
Don we now our gay apparel, Fa la la la la la la la!
Troll the ancient Yuletide carol, Fa la la la la la la la!

See the blazing yule before us, Fa la la la la la la la!
Strike the harp and join the chorus, Fa la la la la la la la!

Follow me in merry measure, Fa la la la la la la la!
While I tell of Yuletide treasure, Fa la la la la la la la!

Fast away the old year passes, Fa la la la la la la la!
Hail the new, ye lads and lasses, Fa la la la la la la la!
Sing we joyous all together! Fa la la la la la la la!

Heedless of the wind and weather, Fa la la la la la la la!

JINGLE BELLS

Dashing through the snow
On a one horse open sleigh
O'er the fields we go,
Laughing all the way
Bells on bob tail ring,
making spirits bright
What fun it is to laugh and sing
A sleighing song tonight

Oh, jingle bells, jingle bells
Jingle all the way
Oh, what fun it is to ride
In a one horse open sleigh
Jingle bells, jingle bells
Jingle all the way
Oh, what fun it is to ride
In a one horse open sleigh

A day or two ago,
I thought I'd take a ride,
And soon Miss Fanny Bright
Was seated by my side;
The horse was lean and lank

Misfortune seemed his lot
We got into a drifted bank,
And then we got upsot.

Oh, jingle bells, jingle bells
Jingle all the way
Oh, what fun it is to ride
In a one horse open sleigh
Jingle bells, jingle bells
Jingle all the way
Oh, what fun it is to ride
In a one horse open sleigh

Jingle Bells, Jingle Bells,
Jingle all the way!
Oh, What fun it is to ride
In a one horse open sleigh.
Jingle Bells, Jingle Bells,
Jingle all the way!
Oh, What fun it is to ride
In a one horse open sleigh.

Now the ground is white
Go it while you're young

Take the girls tonight
And sing this sleighing song
Just get a bob tailed bay
two-forty as his speed
Hitch him to an open sleigh
And crack! you'll take the lead

Jingle Bells, Jingle Bells,
Jingle all the way!
Oh, What fun it is to ride
In a one horse open sleigh.
Jingle Bells, Jingle Bells,
Jingle all the way!
Oh, What fun it is to ride
In a one horse open sleigh.

GRANDMA GOT RUN OVER BY A REINDEER

Grandma got run over by a reindeer
Walking home from our house Christmas eve
You can say there's no such thing as Santa
But as for me and Grandpa, we believe

She'd been drinkin' too much egg nog
And we'd begged her not to go
But she'd left her medication
So she stumbled out the door into the snow

When they found her Christmas mornin'
At the scene of the attack
There were hoof prints on her forehead
And incriminatin' Claus marks on her back

Grandma got run over by a reindeer
Walkin' home from our house Christmas eve
You can say there's no such thing as Santa
But as for me and Grandpa, we believe

Now were all so proud of Grandpa
He's been takin' this so well
See him in there watchin' football
Drinkin' beer and playin' cards with cousin Belle

It's not Christmas without Grandma
All the family's dressed in black
And we just can't help but wonder
Should we open up her gifts or send them back?

Grandma got run over by a reindeer
Walkin' home from our house Christmas eve
You can say there's no such thing as Santa
But as for me and Grandpa, we believe

Now the goose is on the table
And the pudding made of pig
And a blue and silver candle
That would just have matched the hair in
Grandma's wig

I've warned all my friends and neighbors
Better watch out for yourselves
They should never give a license
To a man who drives a sleigh and plays with elves

Grandma got run over by a reindeer
Walkin' home from our house, Christmas eve
You can say there's no such thing as Santa
But as for me and Grandpa, we believe!

O CHRISTMAS TREE

O Christmas tree, O Christmas tree!
How are thy leaves so verdant!
O Christmas tree, O Christmas tree,
How are thy leaves so verdant!

Not only in the summertime,
But even in winter is thy prime.
O Christmas tree, O Christmas tree,
How are thy leaves so verdant!

O Christmas tree, O Christmas tree,
Much pleasure doth thou bring me!
O Christmas tree, O Christmas tree,
Much pleasure doth thou bring me!

For every year the Christmas tree,
Brings to us all both joy and glee.
O Christmas tree, O Christmas tree,
Much pleasure doth thou bring me!

O Christmas tree, O Christmas tree,
Thy candles shine out brightly!
O Christmas tree, O Christmas tree,

Thy candles shine out brightly!

Each bough doth hold its tiny light,
That makes each toy to sparkle bright.
O Christmas tree, O Christmas tree,
Thy candles shine out brightly!

LET IT SNOW

Oh the weather outside is frightful
But the fire is so delightful
And since we've no place to go
Let It Snow! Let It Snow! Let It Snow!

It doesn't show signs of stopping
And I've bought some corn for popping
The lights are turned way down low
Let It Snow! Let It Snow! Let It Snow!

When we finally kiss good night
How I'll hate going out in the storm!
But if you'll really hold me tight
All the way home I'll be warm

The fire is slowly dying
And, my dear, we're still goodbying
But as long as you love me so
Let It Snow! Let It Snow! Let It Snow!

SANTA CLAUS IS COMING TO TOWN

You better watch out
You better not cry
Better not pout
I'm telling you why
Santa Claus is coming to town

He's making a list
And checking it twice
Gonna find out Who's naughty and nice
Santa Claus is coming to town

He sees you when you're sleeping
He knows when you're awake
He knows if you've been bad or good
So be good for goodness sake!

O! You better watch out!
You better not cry
Better not pout
I'm telling you why
Santa Claus is coming to town
Santa Claus is coming to town

SANTA BABY

Santa baby, just slip a sable under the tree for me;
Been an awful good girl, Santa baby
and hurry down the chimney tonight

Santa baby, a '54 convertible too, light blue
I'll wait up for you dear, Santa baby
and hurry down the chimney tonight

Think of all the fun I've missed
Think of all the fellas that I haven't kissed
Next year I could be just as good...
if you'd check off my Christmas list

Santa baby, I want a yacht and really that's not a
lot
Been an angel all year; Santa baby,
so hurry down the chimney tonight

Santa honey, there's one thing I really do need,
the deed - To a platinum mine, Santa baby
so hurry down the chimney tonight

Santa baby, I'm filling my stocking with the

duplex, and checks
Sign your 'X' on the line, Santa cutie,
and hurry down the chimney tonight

Come and trim my Christmas tree
With some decorations bought at Tiffany;
I really do believe in you
Let's see if you believe in me

Santa baby, forgot to mention one little thing, a
ring
I don't mean a phone, Santa baby,
so hurry down the chimney tonight

Hurry down the chimney tonight
Hurry tonight

WHITE CHRISTMAS

I'm dreaming of a White Christmas
Just like the ones I used to know
Where the treetops glisten
and children listen
To hear sleigh bells in the snow.

I'm dreaming of a white Christmas
With every Christmas card I write
May your days be merry and bright
And may all your Christmases be white.

I'm dreaming of a white Christmas
Just like the ones I used to know
Where the treetops glisten
And children listen
To hear sleigh bells in the snow

I'm dreaming of a white Christmas
With every Christmas card I write
May your days be merry and bright
And may all your Christmases be white

THE TWELVE DAYS OF CHRISTMAS

On the first day of Christmas
my true love sent to me:
A Partridge in a Pear Tree

On the second day of Christmas
my true love sent to me:
2 Turtle Doves
and a Partridge in a Pear Tree

On the third day of Christmas
my true love sent to me:
3 French Hens
2 Turtle Doves
and a Partridge in a Pear Tree

On the fourth day of Christmas
my true love sent to me:
4 Calling Birds
3 French Hens
2 Turtle Doves
and a Partridge in a Pear Tree

On the fifth day of Christmas
my true love sent to me:
5 Golden Rings
4 Calling Birds
3 French Hens
2 Turtle Doves
and a Partridge in a Pear Tree

On the sixth day of Christmas
my true love sent to me:
6 Geese a Laying
5 Golden Rings
4 Calling Birds
3 French Hens
2 Turtle Doves
and a Partridge in a Pear Tree

On the seventh day of Christmas
my true love sent to me:
7 Swans a Swimming
6 Geese a Laying
5 Golden Rings
4 Calling Birds
3 French Hens
2 Turtle Doves

and a Partridge in a Pear Tree

On the eighth day of Christmas
my true love sent to me:
8 Maids a Milking
7 Swans a Swimming
6 Geese a Laying
5 Golden Rings
4 Calling Birds
3 French Hens
2 Turtle Doves
and a Partridge in a Pear Tree

On the ninth day of Christmas
my true love sent to me:
9 Ladies Dancing
8 Maids a Milking
7 Swans a Swimming
6 Geese a Laying
5 Golden Rings
4 Calling Birds
3 French Hens
2 Turtle Doves
and a Partridge in a Pear Tree

On the tenth day of Christmas
my true love sent to me:
10 Lords a Leaping
9 Ladies Dancing
8 Maids a Milking
7 Swans a Swimming
6 Geese a Laying
5 Golden Rings
4 Calling Birds
3 French Hens
2 Turtle Doves
and a Partridge in a Pear Tree

On the eleventh day of Christmas
my true love sent to me:
11 Pipers Piping
10 Lords a Leaping
9 Ladies Dancing
8 Maids a Milking
7 Swans a Swimming
6 Geese a Laying
5 Golden Rings
4 Calling Birds
3 French Hens

2 Turtle Doves
and a Partridge in a Pear Tree

On the twelfth day of Christmas
my true love sent to me:
12 Drummers Drumming
11 Pipers Piping
10 Lords a Leaping
9 Ladies Dancing
8 Maids a Milking
7 Swans a Swimming
6 Geese a Laying
5 Golden Rings
4 Calling Birds
3 French Hens
2 Turtle Doves
and a Partridge in a Pear Tree

WINTER WONDERLAND

Sleigh bells ring
are you listening
in the lane
snow is glistening
A beautiful sight
we're happy tonight
walking in a winter wonderland

Gone away is the bluebird
here to stay is a new bird
He sings a love song
as we go along
walking in a winter wonderland

In the meadow we can build a snowman
Then pretend that he is Parson Brown
He'll say: Are you married?
we'll say: No man
But you can do the job
when you're in town

Later on
we'll conspire
as we dream by the fire
To face unafraid
the plans that we've made
walking in a winter wonderland

In the meadow we can build a snowman
and pretend that he's a circus clown
We'll have lots of fun with mister snowman
until the the other kids knock him down

When it snows
ain't it thrilling
Though your nose gets a chilling
We'll frolic and play
the Eskimo way
walking in a winter wonderland

Walking in a winter wonderland
walking in a winter wonderland

O HOLY NIGHT

O Holy Night!
The stars are brightly shining
It is the night of the dear Savior's birth!
Long lay the world in sin and error pining
Till he appear'd and the soul felt its worth.
A thrill of hope the weary soul rejoices
For yonder breaks a new and glorious morn!

Fall on your knees
Oh hear the angel voices
Oh night divine
Oh night when Christ was born
Oh night divine
Oh night divine

Led by the light of Faith serenely beaming
With glowing hearts by His cradle we stand
So led by light of a star sweetly gleaming
Here come the wise men from Orient land
The King of Kings lay thus in lowly manger
In all our trials born to be our friend

Truly He taught us to love one another
His law is love and His gospel is peace
Chains shall He break for the slave is our brother
And in His name all oppression shall cease
Sweet hymns of joy in grateful chorus raise we,
Let all within us praise His holy name

THE LITTLE DRUMMER BOY

Come they told me
Pa rum pum pum pum
A new born King to see
Pa rum pum pum pum

Our finest gifts we bring
Pa rum pum pum pum
To lay before the King
Pa rum pum pum pum,
rum pum pum pum,
rum pum pum pum

So to honor Him
Pa rum pum pum pum
When we come

Little baby
Pa rum pum pum pum
I am a poor boy too
Pa rum pum pum pum
I have no gift to bring
Pa rum pum pum pum
That's fit to give our King

Pa rum pum pum pum,
rum pum pum pum,
rum pum pum pum

Shall I play for you
Pa rum pum pum pum
On my drum

Mary nodded
Pa rum pum pum pum
The ox and lamb kept time
Pa rum pum pum pum
I played my drum for Him
Pa rum pum pum pum
I played my best for Him
Pa rum pum pum pum,
rum pum pum pum,
rum pum pum pum

Then He smiled at me
Pa rum pum pum pum
Me and my drum

IT'S BEGINNING TO LOOK A LOT LIKE CHRISTMAS

It's beginning to look a lot like Christmas
Ev'rywhere you go;
Take a look in the five-and-ten, glistening once
again
With candy canes and silver lanes aglow.

It's beginning to look a lot like Christmas,
Toys in ev'ry store,
But the prettiest sight to see is the holly that will
be
On your own front door.

A pair of hopalong boots and a pistol that shoots
Is the wish of Barney and Ben;
Dolls that will talk and will go for a walk
Is the hope of Janice and Jen;
And Mom and Dad can hardly wait for school to
start again.

It's beginning to look a lot like Christmas
Ev'rywhere you go;
There's a tree in the Grand Hotel, one in the park

as well,
The sturdy kind that doesn't mind the snow.

It's beginning to look a lot like Christmas;
Soon the bells will start,
And the thing that will make them ring is the carol
that you sing
Right within your heart.

JOY TO THE WORLD

Joy to The world! the Lord is come
Let earth receive her King
Let ev'ry heart prepare him room
And heaven and nature sing
And heaven and nature sing
And heaven and nature sing

Joy to the world! the Savior reigns
Let men their songs employ
While fields and floods, rocks, hills and plains
Repeat the sounding joy
Repeat the sounding joy
Repeat the sounding joy

No more let sins and sorrows grow,
Nor thorns infest the ground;
He comes to make His blessings flow
Far as the curse is found,
Far as the curse is found,
Far as, far as, the curse is found.

He rules the world with truth and grace
And makes the nations prove

The glories of His righteousness
And wonders of His love
And wonders of His love
And wonder wonders of His love

WE WISH YOU A MERRY CHRISTMAS

We wish you a Merry Christmas,
We wish you a Merry Christmas,
We wish you a Merry Christmas,
And a Happy New Year.

Good tidings to you,
And all of your kin,
Good tidings for Christmas,
And a Happy New Year.

We all know that Santa's coming,
We all know that Santa's coming,
We all know that Santa's coming,
And soon will be here.

Good tidings to you,
And all of your kin,
Good tidings for Christmas,
And a Happy New Year.

We wish you a Merry Christmas,
We wish you a Merry Christmas,

We wish you a Merry Christmas,
And a Happy New Year

HARK! THE HERALD ANGELS SING

Hark! the herald angels sing,
"Glory to the newborn King!"
Peace on earth, and mercy mild,
God and sinners reconciled
Joyful, all ye nations, rise,
Join the triumph of the skies;
With th' angelic host proclaim,
"Christ is born in Bethlehem."
Hark! the herald angels sing,
"Glory to the newborn King!"

Christ, by highest heav'n adored:
Christ, the everlasting Lord;
Late in time behold him come,
Offspring of the favored one.
Veil'd in flesh, the Godhead see;
Hail, th'incarnate Deity:
Pleased, as man, with men to dwell,
Jesus, our Emmanuel!
Hark! the herald angels sing,
"Glory to the newborn King!"

Hail! the heav'n born Prince of peace!
Hail! the Son of Righteousness!
Light and life to all he brings,
Risen with healing in his wings
Mild he lays his glory by,
Born that man no more may die:
Born to raise the sons of earth,
Born to give them second birth.
Hark! the herald angels sing,
"Glory to the newborn King!"

THE GRINCH THEME SONG
"MR. GRINCH"

You're a mean one, Mr. Grinch
You really are a heel,
You're as cuddly as a cactus, you're as charming as
an eel, Mr. Grinch,
You're a bad banana with a greasy black peel!

You're a monster, Mr. Grinch,
Your heart's an empty hole,
Your brain is full of spiders, you have garlic in
your soul, Mr. Grinch,
I wouldn't touch you with a thirty-nine-and-a-half
foot pole!

You're a foul one, Mr. Grinch,
You have termites in your smile,
You have all the tender sweetness of a seasick
crocodile, Mr. Grinch,
Given a choice between the two of you'd take the
seasick crocodile!

You're a rotter, Mr. Grinch,

You're the king of sinful sots,
Your heart's a dead tomato splotched with moldy
purple spots, Mr. Grinch,
You're a three decker sauerkraut and toadstool
sandwich with arsenic sauce!

You nauseate me, Mr. Grinch,
With a nauseous super "naus"!,
You're a crooked dirty jockey and you drive a
crooked hoss, Mr. Grinch,
Your soul is an appalling dump heap overflowing
with the most disgraceful
assortment of rubbish imaginable mangled up in
tangled up knots!

You're a foul one, Mr. Grinch,
You're a nasty wasty skunk,
Your heart is full of unwashed socks, your soul is
full of gunk, Mr. Grinch,
The three words that best describe you are as
follows, and I quote,
"Stink, stank, stunk"!

I SAW MOMMY KISSING SANTA CLAUS

I saw Mommy kissing Santa Claus
Underneath the mistletoe last night.
She didn't see me creep
down the stairs to have a peep;
She thought that I was tucked
up in my bedroom fast asleep.

Then, I saw Mommy tickle Santa Claus
Underneath his beard so snowy white;
Oh, what a laugh it would have been
If Daddy had only seen
Mommy kissing Santa Claus last night

Then I saw Mommy tickle Santa Claus
Underneath his beard so snowy white
Oh, what a laugh it would have been
If Daddy had only seen
Mommy kissing Santa Claus last night

Oh, what a laugh it would have been
If Daddy had only seen

Mommy kissing Santa Claus last night
(I saw Mommy kissing Santa Claus)

ROCKIN' AROUND THE CHRISTMAS TREE

Rocking around the Christmas Tree
at the Christmas party hop
Mistletoe hung where you can see
Ev'ry couple tries to stop

You will get a sentimental feeling When you hear
voices singing
"Let's be jolly; Deck the halls with boughs of holly"
Rocking around the Christmas Tree
Have a happy holiday
Everyone's dancing merrily
In a new old fashioned way

Rocking around the Christmas Tree
Let the Christmas Spirit ring
Later we'll have some pumpkin pie
and we'll do some caroling

You will get a sentimental feeling When you hear
voices singing
"Let's be jolly; Deck the halls with boughs of holly"
Rocking around the Christmas Tree
Have a happy holiday
Everyone's dancing merrily
In a new old fashioned way

SILENT NIGHT

Silent night, holy night!
All is calm, all is bright.
Round yon Virgin, Mother and Child.
Holy infant so tender and mild,
Sleep in heavenly peace,
Sleep in heavenly peace

Silent night, holy night!
Shepherds quake at the sight.
Glories stream from heaven afar
Heavenly hosts sing Alleluia,
Christ the Savior is born!
Christ the Savior is born

Silent night, holy night!
Son of God love's pure light.
Radiant beams from Thy holy face
With dawn of redeeming grace,
Jesus Lord, at Thy birth
Jesus Lord, at Thy birth

THE FIRST NOEL

The First Noel the angel did say
Was to certain poor shepherds
in fields as they lay;
In fields as they lay, keeping their sheep,
On a cold winter's night that was so deep.

Noel, Noel, Noel, Noel,
Born is the King of Israel.

They looked up and saw a star
Shining in the east beyond them far,
And to the earth it gave great light,

And so it continued both day and night.

And by the light of that same star
Three wise men came from country far;
To seek for a king was their intent,
And to follow the star wherever it went.

This star drew nigh to the northwest,
O'er Bethlehem it took it rest,
And there it did both stop and stay
Right over the place where Jesus lay.

Then entered in those wise men three
Full reverently upon their knee,
and offered there in his presence
Their gold, and myrrh, and frankincense.

Then let us all with one accord
Sing praises to our heavenly Lord;
That hath made heaven and earth of naught,
And with his blood mankind hath bought

FELIZ NAVIDAD

Feliz Navidad
Feliz Navidad
Feliz Navidad
Prospero Ano y Felicidad.

Feliz Navidad
Feliz Navidad
Feliz Navidad
Prospero Ano y Felicidad.

I wanna wish you a Merry Christmas
I wanna wish you a Merry Christmas

I wanna wish you a Merry Christmas
From the bottom of my heart.

Feliz Navidad
Feliz Navidad
Feliz Navidad
Prospero Ano y Felicidad.

Feliz Navidad
Feliz Navidad
Feliz Navidad
Prospero Ano y Felicidad.

I wanna wish you a Merry Christmas
I wanna wish you a Merry Christmas
I wanna wish you a Merry Christmas
From the bottom of my heart.

FROSTY THE SNOWMAN

Frosty the Snowman, was a jolly happy soul,
With a corn cob pipe and a button nose, and two
eyes made of coal.

Frosty the Snowman, is a fairytale, they say.
He was made of snow, but the children know he
came to life one day.

There must have been some magic in that old silk
hat they found,

*For when they placed it on his head, he began to
dance around!*

*Oh, Frosty, the Snowman, was alive as he could
be;
and the children say he could laugh and play,
just the same as you and me.
Thumpety thump, thump, thumpety thump, thump,
look at Frosty go.*

*Thumpety thump, thump, thumpety thump, thump,
over the hills of snow.*

*Frosty the Snowman, knew the sun was hot that
day,
so he said, "Let's run, and we'll have some fun
now, before I melt away."*

*Down to the village, with a broomstick in his
hand,
Running here and there, all around the square,
sayin', "Catch me if you can."*

He led them down the streets of town, right to the

traffic cop;

and only paused a moment, when he heard him
holler, "Stop!"

For Frosty, the Snowman, had to hurry on his
way,
But he waved goodbye, sayin' "Don't cry, I'll be
back again some day."

O COME ALL YE FAITHFUL

O come, all ye faithful,
Joyful and triumphant,
O come ye, O come ye to Bethlehem.
Come and behold Him,
Born the King of Angels!

O come, let us adore Him,
O come, let us adore Him,
O come, let us adore Him,
Christ the Lord.

Sing, alleluia,

All ye choirs of angels;
O sing, all ye blissful ones of heav'n above.
Glory to God
In the highest glory!

O come, let us adore Him,
O come, let us adore Him,
O come, let us adore Him,
Christ the Lord.

Yea, Lord, we greet Thee,
Born this happy morning;
Jesus, to Thee be the glory giv'n;
Word of the Father,
Now in the flesh appearing,

O come, let us adore Him,
O come, let us adore Him,
O come, let us adore Him,
Christ the Lord.

IT'S THE MOST WONDERFUL TIME OF THE YEAR

It's the most wonderful time of the year
With the kids jingle belling
And everyone telling you "Be of good cheer"
It's the most wonderful time of the year
It's the hap-happiest season of all

With those holiday greetings and gay happy
meetings
When friends come to call
It's the hap- happiest season of all

There'll be parties for hosting
Marshmallows for toasting
And caroling out in the snow
There'll be scary ghost stories
And tales of the glories of
Christmases long, long ago

It's the most wonderful time of the year
There'll be much mistletoeing
And hearts will be glowing
When love ones are near
It's the most wonderful time of the year

There'll be parties for hosting
Marshmallows for toasting
And caroling out in the snow
There'll be scary ghost stories
And tales of the glories of
Christmases long, long ago

It's the most wonderful time of the year
There'll be much mistletoeing
And hearts will be glowing
When love ones are near

It's the most wonderful time
It's the most wonderful time
It's the most wonderful time
It's the most wonderful time of the year

A HOLLY JOLLY CHRISTMAS

Have a holly, jolly Christmas;
It's the best time of the year
I don't know if there'll be snow
but have a cup of cheer

Have a holly, jolly Christmas;
And when you walk down the street
Say Hello to friends you know
and everyone you meet

Oh ho

the mistletoe
hung where you can see;
Somebody waits for you;
Kiss her once for me

Have a holly jolly Christmas
and in case you didn't hear
Oh by golly
have a holly jolly Christmas
this yea
{repeats}

About The Author

Osuagwu Malachy Osuagwu Malachy is a content writer with great strategic skill in composition. He is a brainy with lots of God's given gifts; he has written so many inspirational books, engineering, health and life, nature and the likes. He is a twin and they work together. A proud Nigerian with zeal to travelling round the world.